BOOKS BY KENNETH KOCH

POETRY

Straits   1998
One Train   1994
On the Great Atlantic Rainway, Selected Poems 1950–1998   1994
Seasons on Earth   1987
On the Edge   1986
Selected Poems: 1950–1982   1985
Days and Nights   1982
The Burning Mystery of Anna in 1951   1979
The Duplications   1977
The Art of Love   1975
The Pleasures of Peace   1969
When the Sun Tries to Go On   1969
Thank You and Other Poems   1962
Permanently   1961
Ko, or A Season on Earth   1960

FICTION

Hotel Lambosa   1993
The Red Robins   1975

THEATER

The Gold Standard: A Book of Plays   1996
One Thousand Avant-Garde Plays   1988
The Red Robins   1979
A Change of Hearts   1973
Bertha and Other Plays   1966

NONFICTION

Making Your Own Days:
    The Pleasures of Reading and Writing Poetry   1998
Sleeping on the Wing:
    An Anthology of Modern Poetry with Essays on Reading and Writing
    (with Kate Farrell)   1981
I Never Told Anybody:
    Teaching Poetry Writing in a Nursing Home   1977
Rose, Where Did You Get That Red?:
    Teaching Great Poetry to Children   1973
Wishes, Lies, and Dreams:
    Teaching Children to Write Poetry   1970

STRAITS

KENNETH KOCH

Alfred A. Knopf   New York   1998

STRAITS

P O E M S

Library of Congress Cataloging-in-Publication Data

Koch, Kenneth
    Straits : Poems / Kenneth Koch.—1st ed.
    p.   cm.
    ISBN 0-375-40136-9
    I. Title.
PS3521.027 S7   1998   97-50552
811'.54—dc21   CIP

Manufactured in the United States of America
First Edition

Some of these poems originally appeared as follows:

The New York Times: *The Human Sacrament*
The American Poetry Review: *Straits,* and fifteen of the *Songs from the Plays*
Poetry: *Vous Êtes Plus Beaux que Vous ne Pensiez, The Seasons*
The World: *Currency*
The Nation: *The Promenade of the Ghostly Subtitles*
Paris Review: *My Olivetti Speaks*
Yale Review: *Ballade*
PN Review: *Artificial Intelligence*
The New Yorker: two *Songs from the Plays* ("Songs are about death," and "You want a social life with friends")

Some others of the *Songs from the Plays* were previously published, sometimes in different versions, as follows: "Mediterranean suns" in *Hearing,* music by Ned Rorem, published by Boosey & Hawkes, 1968; "If I am to be preserved from heartache and shyness" in *Mostly about Love,* music by Virgil Thomson, published by Schirmer, 1964; "Lo where Haussmann comes, see where he comes" in the opera libretto *Angelica* in *A Change of Hearts,* Random House, 1973; "How in her pirogue she glides," "The Banquet Song," "In Ancient Times," and "Might I be the first" in *The Gold Standard,* Alfred A. Knopf, 1996.

Some sentences and phrases in *Straits* are from two books by Viktor Shklovsky: *The Third Factory,* translated by Richard Sheldon (Ardis Publishers, 1977), and *Mayakovsky and His Circle,* translated by Lily Feiler (Dodd Mead Publishers, 1972).

Currency, three *Songs from the Plays* ("You want a social life with friends," "Your genius made me shiver," and "What makes this statue noble-seeming"), and several sections of *My Olivetti Speaks* were the text of three books made in collaboration with the French artist Bertrand Dorny.

Thanks to Jordan Davis, Harry Ford, and Karen Koch, and
to the Rockefeller Foundation's Bellagio Center

TO BILL AND MARY ANN ELWOOD

CONTENTS

STRAITS

The Human Sacrament

Is nothing new sacred? The book, the sky,
The women on the blue and red screen
Painted in Japan about five hundred years ago. Someone
Has tipped the screen over. I'll set it back up
Putting all the emotion in the thing felt at the thing done. A mirror can
    be clearer
Than a dog, but a small dog can run. Sacred
Is perhaps the relation that caused
My daughter to be born. Yet is she sacred?
She is a woman with someone's arm
Around her shoulders. She is of this world
The way that pipe is, that goes from the well to the house,
And the way the grass is that at this season leaps about up and under it,
And as the cigarette is that the gardener throws in the grass.
Has it a sacred flame? The pipe going to the house. Later, who knows?
The sacred is the sacrament. And it is what
We wanted once to be—
Give me some more coffee,
Some more milk, some more bread, some more breakfast!
Is nothing new sacred? The screen is standing up.
My daughter and her baby come for tea. The baby comes for milk.
They're here in time.

Straits

To Viktor Shklovsky (and containing some of his sentences)

It is easy to be cruel in love: one merely has not to love.
Mayakowsky entered the Revolution as he would his own home. He went right
    in and began opening windows. How serious is it
That something final be accomplished before it is too late?
One entered the earth. One started flinging up diamonds.
They are valuable because they are few not because they are old.
Sitting with Harry in Venice in Loredana's living room
It was easy to be amusing about France. One merely had not to be present
There but in Venice instead. And all that the other guests said to me
How inaccurate or accurate or part of some meaningful or unmeaningful or
    cruel or stupid or worthwhile or happy and life-and-love-giving life they
    seem and related to literature
"A house is at the opera" "Likely it won't be on time," "Town's bridges"
    "I love,"
Wrote Mayakowsky. It was time to disappear into a group of three
And not either be one or a twosome for all eternity.
In this way one could avoid love. Civilization has reached a certain point.
When it had reached a lesser point was the time of one's father
Who seemed a greater point by filling the horizon. Water slopped on the
    walks.
The women wear high-heeled shoes and talk about Christ. "They say he is
    sure to come back." "When?" "I don't know!"
It has never been any man's total destiny to be a father. To this, God may be
    the only exception.
But when God was a man he was a Son.
Many race to be first. Giselle doesn't move. The road passes through oak trees.
    Some trees are pink when in bloom.
New strategies for naval warfare have been worked out
That show that most maneuvers are irrelevant. The most important thing is
    the first engagement.
Gide entered the stables as he would his own home. He went right in and
    began opening gates. It was like a billiards room—with six tables.
A bird may fly through a window directly into a cage.
Bankers are people without a homeland. They live in apartments that look like
    oriental bath houses.
They collect china and occasionally say something witty. We are pleased when
    they come to visit us. The days pass away like a shower.

They are accompanied by actresses, who say, "The world is a gentle place."
I will never marry. Oh but you must marry. It's the only way to bear a
    legitimate son.
An illegitimate son is fine with me. I don't want to marry. It is easy to lie down
    on the stones.
The knife craves a throat. The hangman's noose is giddier than a razor.
She goes away. When he comes back to meet her the curtains are yellow.
They are folded, in pleats. You say to me "It is all over." It is all over
    at home.
As soon as you say "It is not all over" it is no longer all over at home.
We had to hoist a sail into a new wind. The movie star and the novelist
Are dead still not knowing anything, the scientist who improved our lives
And the German shepherd also who brought us delight for years.
Windows are broken and some have been boarded over. It is easy to be a
    glazier to the young
Harder to be a plasterer to the old. Not only the strong but the weak leave a
    legacy. They show life is not gone
When half gone. The man with the broken leg in the swimming pool is an
    encouraging sight. It is Andy.
Andy is it really safe for you to be swimming alone today? Yes, he replies. I am
    looking for a strait,
A way from this pool into the sea. If he cannot have everything, he will have
    something.
The birds also found it possible to make an adjustment. They took fresh views
    of the clouds.
One flew over here, one flew under there. An orchestra conductor raised his
    glove
To throw it to a woman in the first row. The city was sunny because no smoke
    rose from the chimneys.
Unchallenged, everyone remained alive. Once the boat started moving, some
    did not.
He saw the old way of life as a bunker that had to be stormed.
Do you remember the idea "Revolution"? planning for and waiting for the
    revolution?
A painter took over Venice's outdoor cafés as his own private particular province.
This was true for three and a half months even though his paintings were not
    very good
By objective standards. For a while he had a certain panache.
The world lives through long periods of drudgery so it can enjoy one splendid
    space.
The great, dutiful buildings had no tendency to fall down. But one bomb or
    one rocket

5

Could change their sunny adolescence. What building cares if it is knocked
     down?

The facade longs for a bombshell, the infrastructure for an air raid.

It was daylight in the apartment. I usually visited there in the evening.

Magellan sailed along the shore of America, looking for straits.

He sailed into the wide estuaries of rivers, but there he found that it was
     fresh water.

Fresh water meant no straits. Straits would be filled with salt water. But there
     were bays.

Magellan solved his problem of circling America but he didn't return home
     alive. He went in and began testing estuaries.

At noon he was on a coastline looking for a channel to another ocean. Vales of
     rocks. But there are bays. They are panoramas.

Magellan had to hoist a new sail. Once it was hoisted he had to find a briny
     path.

The wind roars like a madman. Magellan goes to sleep. When he wakes up it
     is the Pacific.

Birds stand on the deck. They are Indians.

One does not die of love unrequited but of ceasing to love. Chaliapin sings.
     The audience sits down.

The Zairians sold the machinery from the Belgian coppermines. No more
     copper could be pulled from the earth.

Belgians had to be called back. Their cruelty was equaled only by their mining
     expertise. They were nasty colonialists but good miners.

The sun shines on the rolling water and also on the marble tiles. The penguins
     were replaced by Indians.

We are looking for a shortcut.

The tree doesn't exist in a metaphysical world. The roots crave water, the
     trunk is ready for an axe.

At that time I was a Futurist.

Mark Twain loved his double, Huck Finn. He loved him more than
     himself.

He never did renounce him. When Hyperion wakes up the world is already
     full of sun.

Nonetheless it doesn't seem true what a Swiss banker said to me in Haute
     Savoie one evening: "Banking is just like poetry."

There were painted red tiles. Here and there were interspersed some blue
     ones. A few were green or white.

The sky was old by then: the morning and evening papers were
     interchangeable.

One gives money for a work by Velasquez—not to pay Velasquez for the time
     he spent painting the work

But to pay the countless others who couldn't do it—to cover their costs.

We have to find straits but instead we find intelligence.

Why did you hurt your leg? Freud asks his son.

The moon rises over the inland ocean even on revolutionary holidays.

In love, as in art, we pay for failures. We thank one individual for the success of humanity.

Freud's son didn't know what to say to his father. Other people's troubles are easy to bear.

Neither the bankers nor the women they went out with were interested in marriage. They thought it the ruin of love.

Mayakowsky was sure of himself as long as he was in action.

Unable to break out of his style of painting, Velasquez painted five hundred canvases.

Eventually his stylistic problem was solved—by another painter.

The actor started speaking words as if they were his own

And not those of Shakespeare or of de Montherlant or of Chaliapin.

Looking up at the hilly shore, he saw the fires made by Indians.

He supposed a name for the peninsula: Tierra del Fuego.

But what if it were not a peninsula? The birds might then be presumed to go further away.

They were used to seeing it only in the afternoon.

"With these you can start a new life." She gave him her jewels.

Conversation is one thing in the South and another in the North.

In the North one keeps moving.

In China, they risked banishment or prison if they talked. This then was changed but not completely changed.

The opening up of freedom takes place in steps:

First one speaks of the ocean, then of the boats, then of the people on the boats, lastly of their ideas.

The fishstore man praises the young woman's smile and her clothing. What munitions makers do is to diversify. There are annuals.

Magellan sent an Indian boy to pick some before they had faded; when he came back,

Magellan had decided. "We'll call it Tierra del Fuego."

The sun rose high over the fourth or fifth inland ocean he had seen. At home in Europe he had been a shy student,

Thought lazy and not very good with girls. When he set off, however,

Flags from every nation and of every color adorned the flagpoles

And the tallest masts of the highest ships of the world. And Magellan went

As Mayakowsky went, and as Mark Twain and Cicero went, into the future.

　　He stood on a promontory.

Bankers predicted flax was on the rise and, with it, maize and broccoli.

It's not true that all predictions are false. But it is true that those who make
   them don't know if they are or not.
Pushkin and Lermontov and Gogol waited on the bookshelf for
   Mayakowsky—
If people were on the moon, they could have seen, for one second, a new
   world.
Then just as suddenly Mayakowsky re-became a book; his covers were like
   penguins.
The hot vibrations of his poetry flamed and calmed down. They wandered
   around the apartments
Looking for girls who spoke their own language. Some were fond of saying,
You don't really need to know more than a few words, maybe not even that.
Ponce de Leon noticing his graying beard in the mirror
Said, "I know what I have to find!" He set off, but he never found the
   Fountain of Youth.
Poniatowsky once found something he thought resembled it: a railroad station.
He was fascinated by the choice of different directions. But he aged anyway.
   By then Ponce de Leon was gone.
He imagines a woman who is like a strait, into a cold happiness, which is like a
   sea.
Cranes looking down see only fragments, gay Twombly-like interrupted
   scrambles.
Thenceforth we didn't write our work in regular lines
But in staffs, like music. Satie came out and sat at the mendicant's door.
Gandhi said, "I didn't know I had a door! Now I need no longer be
   wandering!"
They were waiting for a foot; and, after the foot, a leg; and then a staff.
Life brims with music when a country is founded
Or merges with another, or is diversified, like the Dionne Quintuplets. Cicero
   gave his best speeches
When he was a drunk, and Horace wrote his finest poems. There were no
   brothels: property tax had gone up.
Zeus was not a god but a projection of human consciousness. We live in the
   consequences
Of what we imagine persons like Gandhi have done.
The portholes looked like windows of a shop in which they were selling the
   ocean—
How much do you want for this? how much for that?
Eskimos are amazed at the size of the apartments. They think that they must
   be places to keep the dogs.
They are uninterested in politics but fascinated by the apartments.
No casino was opened because no one was rich—

One night's losses could ruin a person for the rest of his or her life.

For Poniatowsky, gambling was displaced to love—also for everyone he knew.

Bankers invested heavily in Magellan's voyage and their money was never paid
back.

They invested in something that might pay off centuries in the future.

Magellan returned dead although he had circled South America.

One banker's girlfriend walked in freezing weather all the way from another
district

To see Mayakowsky. But he was never at home. She installed herself in his
apartment.

Her banker came there looking for her; she met him at the door.

She said, "There is no going backward in a revolution. A revolution is like a
devaluation of currency.

It is what it is and it happens when it happens." He said "You will never win
the love of Mayakowsky."

She said that that however was what she wanted.

The idea of installing a phone booth to some seemed central.

People wished to communicate. The sight of a phone booth was like a whiff of
salt air, from the sea.

The plan of having a Doge as governor was quickly abandoned—it was
impractical

From every point of view. The china belonged to an admiral. Forty-five years
ago he had gone to school

With Yesenin's father. He had padded shoulders, like a football player; he was
sturdy but short.

We came to see him to ask help for an artistic project; he was amiable but
unresponsive.

In a civilization one has to be Mark Twain or André Eglevsky or, at the limit,
Lord Byron.

Shakespeare looked in a mirror. It was much more bracing to open a window:

There one could see only what one was not. Prospero found Ferdinand as a
husband for Miranda.

Once Shakespeare had written the play the subject was dead.

I had seen the apartment only in the afternoon or early evening.

Once I had done that, it was easier to see what had to be done.

Music didn't sound to Orpheus as it did to Rilke. Orpheus took it for granted

As a natural thing and an accompaniment to words. Parliament was convened.

"When were you here last?" Napoleon whispered to his horse.

When his horse didn't reply, Napoleon smiled, and rode him into battle.

When his horse died, he wept.

I didn't know you were living near this pool! "Oh, I don't," said Andy; "to
swim here I come a long way

Past shops and market stalls—I am looking for a strait." But there is none
    in this pool, Andy. Humanity is astonished
By the successes it contains and tends to celebrate the failures
Until a new explanation comes to light.
Mayakowsky imagined he saw a wolf in the long Moscow night
But actually he committed suicide. The deed was signed but no one had
    looked at the property.
The sun went into the west opening up portholes. These were stars
At which you could buy the Ascension.
Books were a scarcity. A man would fold up a newspaper and read it as a book.
    The ice lasted
Until spring. The orchestra was conducted
By a former slave but everyone was free when Chaliapin sang. During the
    Cold War
Forgetfulness was almost a necessity, it was difficult to live without it.
I made friends with a member of the Russian embassy. I asked him if he was
    an attaché or the ambassador.
The Russian only nodded grimly and walked into the canal.
The newspapers next day reported Mayakowsky's death
As an accident. The Apollos had an "archaic smile"—one theory was that
    there existed a happiness
At that time in that place that never existed anyplace else.
Wallace Stevens thought to find it in Florida, taking the boat
Across the Gulf to Havana, where he would find compliant young women.
    This was the source of many of his poems.
El Greco lived in Seville but wasn't a Spaniard
But a Greek. As was the case with Christ, his name designated what, not who,
    he was.
There was a phone booth about every half mile. Magellan had an address book
With nothing in it. He had burned all his past relationships. He might not
    have recognized Chaliapin
As a great singer. But he was going to the South Pole
Whether anyone wanted him to or not. The "archaic smile" is attributed by
    others,
Like Disney's use of four-fingered gloves, to the relative easiness of making
    things that way, a smile is easier to draw
Than a ruminative or prescient expression. A proletarian navy
Seemed a contradiction, like ordinary eyes with an avant-garde nose.
One had to be a "Lombardi" to work on the church. He wanted to detain
    autumn.
It was departing. It took the drapes down from the trees,
Threw everything on the floor, started packing.

Autumn was holding its gun to the head of the willows.
The streetcar tracks brought syphilis to the door. Tall and sometimes blissful
She was running around his apartment dressed in fabric.
At the end of the month, when the rent came due, she got on a bus
And went to the Vatican. The linden's leaves dried. A notice came again
For the rent. Convicted intellectuals were confined to a room and allowed only
    one book per month.
The captain changed into a dinner jacket. On holidays, the villagers would
    choose up sides and fight.
Walt Whitman wrote, There was never any more perfection than there is now.
When he looked out the window he saw the sun.
Poetry burned on tables. Whitman wrote flattering reviews of himself. A
    German scholar
Who up till that time had been a fervent admirer, changed, when he found this
    out,
And became a ferocious detractor. He confused what Whitman was with what
    Whitman wrote.
If Giselle lay down, the people danced over her. She has on a vest of aqua.
But there are bays. Andy is carving his way through one of them, hand over
    hand.
The Doge acknowledged that trade was bad. He went back in and began
    opening up trade routes.
Later he was deposed, an old man who was too fond of young women. But no
    one else could be found at his level.
Venice remained ungoverned for forty years. It could thank one of its leaders
    for the success of its trade routes.
When the rat came out from behind the curtain it seemed no longer a rat
But it was—it just happened that the sunlight had disguised it as a ball of
    yarn.
It was easy to be a signer of the Constitution. One merely had to be there.
Youth gave power to some people, and money gave power to others.
Some spent their youth devising theories, others on experiencing sex
With as many persons as possible. Only a small minority were fascinated by
    estuaries.
Music was defined by Tchaikowsky as "disappearing youth." When he wrote
    music, it stopped disappearing.
The ocean is a source of elegies and a popular location for casinos.
There wasn't money for people to spend on taking taxis. The taxi drivers
    didn't blame them.
They felt, correctly, that they were stuck in a proletarian society
With providing an aristocratic mode of transportation. They took their
    plight with some humor.

Occasionally a banker took a cab and spent a lot of money. He was paying not
    for the ride he got
But for the availability of the service. What if the revolution were like a taxi
And couldn't be afforded? We say that life is beautiful
Not only to pay a compliment to something in which we are already included
But to separate inside and outside, if only for a moment.
Shklovsky said, "I speak in a voice grown hoarse from silence and pamphlets."
It didn't pay him to be wrong about the Soviet State and it didn't pay him to
    be right.
He said, "Spring was creeping under coats and over bosoms," and "Quiet
    and fat, I ran around in a shiny black jacket."
With style, he opposed the state. "Death is not the worst of all sorrows," said
    the Italian
Who came to fix Shklovsky's clock. This clock was stuck at quarter after
    eleven.
Elsa didn't call back. He spoke of the factory.
No one was supposed to comment on the failings of Soviet industry.
Putilov has an area of fifty square miles and a population of thirty-five
    thousand.
Most of these people work in the plant. The plant makes a tremendous
    amount of noise but produces very little.
The machines are out-of-date and not well taken care of. Thus the clatter.
Mayakowsky opened windows. Shklovsky wrote,
"Noise is work for an orchestra, but not for the Putilov plant."
He spent a number of years in exile. "It is supposed to be turning out
    products."

Vous Êtes Plus Beaux que Vous ne Pensiez

1

Botticelli lived
In a little house
In Florence
Italy
He went out
And painted Aphrodite
Standing on some air
Above a shell
On some waves
And he felt happy
He
Went into a café
And cried
I'll buy
Everybody a drink
And for me
A punt e mes
Celebrities thronged
To look at his painting
Never had anyone seen
So beautiful a painted girl
The real girl he painted
The model
For Aphrodite sits
With her chin in her hand
Her hand on her wrist
Her elbow
On a table
And she cries,
"When I was
Naked I was believed,
Will be, and am."

2

Sappho lived
In a little house
Made out of stone
On the island
In Greece of Lesbos
And she lived
To love other women
She loved girls
She went out
And was tortured by loving someone
And then was
Tortured by
Loving someone else
She wrote great
Poems
About these loves
Poems so great
That they actually seem
Like torture themselves
Torture to know
So much sweetness
Can be given
And can be taken away.

3

George Gordon Lord Byron lived
In a little house
In England
He came out
Full of fire
And wild
Creative spirits
He got himself in trouble all the time
He made love to his sister
He was a devil to his wife
And she to him!
Byron was making love
Part of the time
In ottava rima
And part of the time
Really
Teresa Guiccioli lived
In a big palace
In Venice
And Byron made love to her
Time after time after time.

4

Saint Francis of Assisi lived
In a little house
Full of fine
And expensive things
His father
Was a billionaire
(SIR Francis of Assisi)
And his mother was a lady
Most high and rare
Baby Francis stayed there
And then he went out
He found God
He saw God
He gave all
His clothes away
Which made
His father mad
Very mad
Saint Francis gave
To poor
People and to animals
Everything he had
Now he has a big church
Built to him in Assisi
His father has nothing
Not even
A mound of earth
With his name
SIR
FRANCIS OF ASSISI
Above it
Carved on a stone.

5

Borges lived
In a little house
In Buenos Aires.
He came out
And wrote
Stories, and
When he was blind
Was director
Of the National Library
La Biblioteca Nacional.
No one at the library
Knew he was a famous man.
They were amazed
At the elegant women
Who came to pick him up—
Like a book!—
At the Library day's end!

6

Vladimir Mayakowsky lived
In a little house
In Russia
He came out
And painted pictures
And wrote poems:
"To the Eiffel Tower"
"To My Passport"
"At the Top of My Lungs"
"A Cloud in Trousers"—
Before he died—
Was it suicide
Or was he murdered
By the Secret Police—
Crowds of fifty thousand gathered
To hear him read his lines.

7

Maya Plisetskaya lived
In a little house
In Russia
There was snow
All around
And often
For weeks at a time
Maya Plisetskaya's feet
Didn't touch the ground
The way, afterwards,
They never seemed to touch
The stage
She said The age
When you begin
To understand dance
Is the same
As that at which
You start to lose
Your elevation.

8

Ludwig Wittgenstein lived
In a little house
In Vienna
He came out
And went to live
In another house
In England
He kept coming out
And going back in
He wrote philosophy
Books that showed
We do not know how we know
What we mean
By words like Out and In.
He was revered like a god
For showing this
And he acted like a god
In mid-career
He completely changed his mind.

9

Frank O'Hara lived
In a little house
In Grafton, Massachusetts
Sister and brother
Beside him.
He took out
Toilet articles from his house
And he took out
Candles and books
And he took out
Music and pictures and stones
And to himself he said
Now you are out
Of the house Do something
Great! He came
To New York
He wrote "Second Avenue," "Biotherm"
And "Hatred."
He played the piano
He woke up
In a construction site
At five a.m., amazed.

Jean Dubuffet lived
In a little house
In the south of France
He came out
And made paintings
He went back in
And made some more
Soon Jean Dubuffet had
A hundred and five score
He also did sculptures,
And paintings
That were like sculptures
And even some sculptures
That were like
Paintings Such
Is our modern world
And among the things
He did
Was a series
Of portraits
Of his artist and writer
Friends A large series
Entitled You Look
Better than You Thought You
Did Vous Êtes
Plus Beaux que
Vous ne Pensiez.

Study of Time

One bird deserves another. One white and orange tabletop.
One twenty-five-year-old deserves another
Twenty-five-year-old. One harlequin deserves another harlequin. One rich
  cocktail of flames deserves another
And one extravagant boast: I am the Obvious. My hunch is me.
One brain deserves a brain that has been hatched in the tropics
One broken heart a heart that has been differently broken.
It seems to me time to get something done. But if I get in the car
I am forty-five years old and you are nineteen. We are
Not going anywhere. The car won't start. And if I get out
I am sixty years old. I look around but don't see you there.
I expect it's a good presumption that you are coming back,
But hurry. If I go into the drugstore
I am thirty-three. The boy behind the counter
Is not a girl, but we discuss national politics anyway.
That fucking Nixon. Or That damned unholy war! If I read a magazine
At the stand, on the other side of the drugstore,
I am twenty-five, and you, dressed with some hoop-la, come in.
I am sixteen when I am lying on the floor, with you beside me
Reading a newspaper. One stone man
Deserves one stone woman, and one glad day of being alone
And in good health. If at seventy
I get up and close the door,
I am fourteen and you are twenty. I'll put on
My blue shirt. My white tie, I'm twenty, twenty-one. Now we are eighty.
One five o'clock sunny day
Deserves another. We are both fifty-four. You pick up the bar that holds the
  door
And hit it as hard as you can at twenty. The floor deserves the floor
Of heaven that is a ceiling as we see it. One coldly affected group
Deserves another. We both very much enjoy engaging in sports.
You fall down, I pick you up. I am eight
You are sixty-six. Today is your birthday. You stand opening a cantaloupe. You
  say, Let's
Try another! You are sitting in the car,

You are twenty-three, I am forty-four and singing a Spanish song.
If she is nine years old, then I am fifty.
The birthdays come and go talking of Prospero. Good-bye, house!
Do you remember when we used to live in you
And be forty-eight years old? One age deserves another. One time deserves
    another time.

Currency

In the Fifties Western Europe was the place
That had just been through a war. The currencies were wobbly.
A run-down American student could live like Wallace Stevens
Among the moguls of Hartford. This was helpful for poetry
If bad for a lot else. Not many French apartments had bathrooms,
Almost none refrigerators. One went to the public baths and looked out
The already steamed-up windows at the city.
I sat around a lot in Montparnasse
Cafés—you know them, the Select, the Dôme, and
The Rotonde. The Rotonde those days stayed open
All night. The old-fashioned French coffee machine was steaming.
It gave off an awful and awfully exciting smell.
The Surrealists were aging, like the paper of their books
Le paysan de Paris and Les malheurs des immortels
Above—up there—the river is winding. The museum is full of busts
Its large paintings are like days.
A friend was foreign and far away.
Everyone understands these things but no one is looking.
The fire escapes are in New York with everyone else.
Important here is to get my foot on the street
Before the car gets there. From the asphalt gas and steam not going up.
However, there is a book store on the rue de Rennes.
Its French books are very cheap.
A book costs hardly more than a postcard in the United States.
This situation is temporary. Meanwhile I am becoming well-read
In modern French poetry. I also read La Chanson de Roland translated into
        Modern French
And Virgil's Eclogues and his Georgics translated into French.
They seem to make more sense to me than in English.
I find it in the air as well as in Max Jacob,
In Jouve and in de Montherlant. Surrealism is bouquet to these arrogated
        French tables.
Who thinks about those things.
I am away from ghostly and boasting New York.
In the bookstore I meet Henri Michaux. The kind man who owns the
        bookstore introduces me to him
He thinks we may both like it

I more than Henri Michaux. I like it.
I am nervous I am some kind of phantom.
No don't buy the Larousse buy this a truly serious dictionary a man under the
    sidewalk in his papery dusty crowded store says to me
But I am not that scholarly American
I am learning from Paris's streets to lead a life without consequence
But isn't that a life of consequence?
It is not very often that I get around to love-making
Not in this first early year.
Sexual passion and excitement are more interesting to me when I am older.
They interested me every year.
I am not studying this but Je t'aime and je vais jouir
I'm learning French phrases but I feel mystified and off to the side
I notice her long thin arms she wants to be an airline stewardess
If I held on long enough I'd be perhaps somewhat "French"
I want to be famous amidst the prose of everyday existence
In fact this year I don't care about fame
I have never cared about it I just want to be delighted and I'm envious
I want to be part of that enormous cake over there
That is a monument being wheeled down les Champs Elysées
I am daft about Paris's white sidewalks
Everything I have read and done since then
Is not more real. I wrote I completely forget what.
One friend said this version (#2) is "more abstract" than this (1st) one. I said
    Thank you.
Michaux was pleasant with me, and witty.
Invisible the monstrous sufferer of his poetry
Whereas my overexcited feeling is all too evident.
I am twenty-five years old and in good health sleeping
I'm sitting in a smoky restaurant
Thanksgiving Day Sixth Arrondissement I was not eating turkey
Or cranberry sauce but some petits suisses
These are very petits but are they suisses in what ways are they suisses
The conversation's booming around me
I feel lost in this breaking ocean of French happiness-inducing culinary
    indulgence
These fat bourgeois I am a thin bourgeois only because I am twenty-five
Giacometti is sitting drinking at the Dôme. He is with his followers.
I have a bicycle. I try but I can't hear one word that Giacometti says.
How long ago is it that I started to "dream in French"? Two months.
I want to be something else. I keep listening.
Life isn't infinite.

Now it may seem infinite but it isn't infinite.
Minor ailments don't interfere with my struggle to become French.
I will never become French.
I like too much being American. Also partly French.
Jean Cocteau equals Juan Gris. They even have, almost, the same name.
Birds ce sont les oiseaux.
Here I am in Paris being miserably lonely. All the same.
All the same even Amadis de Gaul knew when it was time to go home.
When he had conquered his enemies.
I have not yet conquered France.
By the time I get close to it I think death may have conquered me.
My first "moment" on French soil which is the soil of Normandy
The ship the Degrasse lands and I put down my foot
On some sparsely grown grass mud that leads up to the platform where the
    train
Is that will be taking me to Paris
To Montparnasse its beds are its streets
Its pillows the cafés. I am streetless in the Hotel de Fleurus
Then I came down from there.
My mail is at American Express.
I have a friend who will not be my friend for very long.
And many, unknown, I have yet to meet.
What will it matter? It matters that I am not alone.
It matters that someone agrees
And that there are walls like energy.
I am unaware of a lot that has gone on here—the herding of the Jews
Into railroad cars, to Belsen.
I read Max Jacob "La rue Ravignan" in
Le cornet à dés with its conclusion "c'est toi, Dostoievski"
In the road I pick up leaves in the street I pick up books
Max Jacob who had long ago proofread the last page of his *The Central
    Laboratory*
Is dead, killed by the Nazis.
Now Larry like a clown down the street
It's extremely late and Nell we three meet
And drink coffee
It tastes like dirt or metal, hot and steaming, like the whole world that's
    coming to be,
The coffee of our lives, the strong and bitter café de nos vies.
The yellow and pink lines come marching down the boulevard Montparnasse
We can pay for the coffee so we have the dawn.

My Olivetti Speaks

Birds don't sing, they explain. Only human beings sing.

If half the poets in the world stopped writing, there would still be the same amount of poetry.

If ninety-nine percent of the poets in the world stopped writing poetry, there would still be the same amount of poetry. Going beyond ninety-nine percent might limit production.

The very existence of poetry should make us laugh. What is that all about? What is it for?

Oxford and Cambridge, two great English universities, are based on poetry. If poetry vanished, they would fall down.

Olive likes poetry but Popeye doesn't. Popeye says, "Swee'pea is poetry for me." Popeye is making a familiar mistake. Human beings and poems are entirely different things. But, claims Popeye, Swee'pea is not a human being. He am a cartoon. It may be that Swee'pea is a poem but he is not exactly written. He is a calligramme without words. It is quite possible to like such kinds of poems but I prefer the others, the regular ones, written out.

In the old days a good place to publish a poem was the *Partisan Review*. Heady—among those thick, heavy pages—one felt ranked by the rankers, a part of the move, a part of the proof—toward what? of what? To find out, you had to read countless *Partisan Review*s. Then you would see what it was. You could be as serious as Delmore Schwartz, as serious as anyone who ever lived. He consistently turned down my poems. I loved that magazine. It weighed an intellectual ton. What would a poem of mine have been doing inside it anyway? How could it have fitted into that heavy and amazing vision of contemporary life?

Sex is to poetry as sex is to everything else. It forgives it, but it also forgets it even while it is planning it.

"I don't like it but I know it is a great poem." I feel the same way about you.

"Poetry is making a comeback." But why is it always bad poetry, or a false idea about poetry, that is making a comeback? I don't think good poetry has ever made a comeback, or ever will. That's one reason it's necessary to keep on writing it.

A dog barks in rhyme but the rhyme is never planned by the dog. This is not a value judgment in any way but it may be an introduction to the consideration of the aesthetic pleasures of being and not being a dog.

Rhyme was very good. Then rhyme was very bad. Then it was forbidden. Then, leader of a rebellion, it came back. Now it has grown old and mellowed, no longer smokes cigars, is less militant, seems sinking into acceptance of parliamentary democracy (to a degree!), and a poet can use it or not, pretty much as he or she chooses. However, anyone who uses it has to be careful, extra-careful, he doesn't get shot. No old-fashioned communism, if you please! Use it and get out. Use it and run. Probably more quickly than anything else, rhyme can show how self-uninformed you are.

On the island of rhymesters, anyone who is any good is king. It's a rare talent. Statues of Byron, Ariosto, Petrarch, and Herrick on the coast are misleading. In the interior, there are no statues at all.

A short life and one hundred good poems. A long life and two good poems. No one has ever had to make this choice.

Here is someone talking about poetry. The only people who listen are those who don't know anything about poetry and those who do.

Shakespeare was the last great poet of the Middle Ages. Keats was the first great poet of Modern Times. Each poet alive now is both desirous of, and afraid of, being the last.

"I bring fresh showers for thirsting flowers." Poetry sometimes seems part of an enormous game of Fill in the Blanks. Let every emotion, idea, sensation be covered (filled in) and may none escape. When we have totally completed this board, when all is color, line, and shading, no blank spaces at all, we may, then, see what this great solved jigsaw puzzle means. (I already have one idea: the refreshment of childhood grossly modified by social and historical change.) The Last Judgment is nothing compared to what then we shall see! Otherwise (if there is no puzzle of this sort) why is Shelley disguising himself as a cloud? Wouldn't that be a waste of time?

The awakening of sexual feelings in a hedgehog is a poetic subject possibly not yet covered. This doesn't imply, however, that we should concentrate our efforts on covering it, though someone may, and if he is as good a poet as Ronsard, and has a thriving tradition behind him, he may do it well.

The last century was full of music, as this one has been full of painting. Poetry, complexly amused, has been content to take second place in both.

Byron was so unlikely ever to write a sonnet that people in his time used to say, when they were skeptical about a thing, "Oh, sure, like Byron's sonnet!" A seemingly impossible windfall, any staggeringly unlikely event was called a "Byron's sonnet." When someone proposed removing all the Carpaccio paintings from Venice, the witty Doge Meduno Rabanatti is reported to have said, "Certainly! as soon as we get Byron's sonnet in exchange." Byron, according to one story, hearing of this conversation, immediately sat down and wrote a sonnet, which—since he loved the Carpaccios and wanted them to stay—he then just as immediately tore up.

Nostalgia for old poetry is like nostalgia for Ancient Egypt—one is hardly lamenting one's own youth. Imagine an Egyptian youth and that he speaks to you. Who is that lovely young woman by his side? No one you have ever hurt with your fear or your false promises, that's sure. Dissolution may not be so bad, if only it didn't need to be preceded by death, as it isn't in poetry.

A glass breaks when someone sings a high note, and when someone makes a great breakthrough in a poem there is a stranger in the mirror.

To read a poem we sit down; to look at a painting we stand up. Art is always saying hello and poetry is always saying good-bye. It says, Your dreams are leaving town, and not even Byron can prevent it, nor any other Lord.

To look at a painting we stand up because of our voracity. We don't want anyone else getting it before us, not the slightest part. We are quickly satisfied, however, given how strong this voracity is. We soon move away. Reading a poem we don't mind interruptions. That poem will be there when we come back. Still, we don't want someone reading over our shoulder.

I will live in that little house with you and write poetry! This statement, taken in isolation from all others, and from all the rest of reality, is wonderful and touching to think about.

Yes! I will write too! Already the situation is less "ideal." This means two quiet places and two typewriters. And as for the house—

Five great poets writing about five different things constitute a Renaissance. Five great poets writing about the same thing constitute a "school" (une école).

A mermaid who recites poetry is a lost mermaid.

A curious thing about the wind is that one can't tell if its music is ever the same, because one never hears the beginning.

Write poetry as if you were in love. If you are always in love you will not always write the same poem, but if you are never in love, you may.

The relation of emotion to poetry is like that of squirrels to a tree. You don't live in what you never have to leave.

"The most modern person in Europe is you Pope Pius the Tenth," Apollinaire wrote in 1913. Being modern was equivalent to being surprising—for about twenty years (1908–1928).

To be ahead of everything and still to be behind in love—a predicament poets may imagine they are in.

That person in the corner has published poems!—A marvel for youth.

My brother-in-law here is a poet.—Leap out the door! Though the brother-in-law may be a much better poet than that person in the corner. Or they may be the same one.

This poem is worth more than these emeralds and diamonds. How can that possibly be? there is no monetary value to a poem. To this one there is: I set the price myself.

I know for sure that I am not a calligramme. When I look at my arms or my hands or my legs, there are no comments, they aren't formed by letters of words. From birth to death I remain unexplained—at least in that manner.

The first poem one writes is usually not the worst. It is not like one's first kiss or one's first time driving a car but more like one's first success.

Ice is like prose; fire is like poetry. But neither melts nor goes out. Ideally (or unideally, some would say) they generally ignore each other's existence.

Rhyme is like a ball that bounces not in the same place but at least in another place where it can bounce.

Poets who write every day also write every year, which is the important thing for poetry.

The poet is the unacknowledged impersonator of the greatest unborn actors of his time.

The Romantic movement left, when it departed, a tremendous gap in poetry which could be filled by criticism and by literary theory but which would be better left alone.

Rome inspired architects and sculptors and painters; the Lake Country inspired poets. Milton inspired Keats. Perugino taught Raphael. Blake gave ideas to Yeats. Sciascia read *Chroniques italiennes* once every year. Byron learned something from Pope. Even the most unsentimental person is glad to see his home country again.

A tapestry is not like a lot of little poems woven together but like one big poem being taken apart.

Starting off as an Irish poet, one has a temperamental and geographical advantage. Starting off as a French poet, one incites an overwhelming curiosity as to what can be done. Starting off as an American poet, one begins to develop a kind of self-consciousness that may quickly lead to genius or to nothing.

Would that he had blotted a thousand! "Perfection" is wonderful in poetry but Shakespeare is good enough—one reads on!

There are three Testaments and one is illegible.

The iris is a flower that is past meridian, a ghost come bearing you a villanelle.

What is the matter with having a subject? Wittgenstein says, "There are no subjects in the world; a subject is a limitation of the world." In fact our subject is all around us like a mail-order winter that we carelessly sent in a request for when it seemed it would always be spring.

Eve was the first animal. Therefore she could not have been Eve, and Adam could not have written poetry. Adam could not write poetry unless there was a human Eve. Thousands of years later, there was: Eve de Montmorency. But she didn't encourage the production of poetry. She said I'll kill anyone who writes me a poem. I like life to be real! Inspired, all the same, a few poets began writing "free verse" (and it was pretty good) which she was unable to recognize as poetry. Meanwhile, back in the Garden of Eden, Eve woke up. She was a fox no more, but a woman, and a ravishing one! Adam saw her and became terribly excited. Without willing to or wishing to at all (for who could know the consequences?) he fell to one knee before her, held out his hands and recited: Roses are red, violets are blue. Yes, what's the rest? Eve said. I don't know, Adam said. I'm not yet fully a poet. That's as far as I've got. So far so good, Eve said, and she loved him with a new ardency that night. From their union were born Abel and Cain, who represented two dissenting schools of criticism: Abel, the "inspirational," let-yourself-go, just SAY it, let it all hang out, or blossom! Lyrical School; Cain, the party of more rigorously crafted delight, a sylvan Valéry: l'inspiration n'est pour rien—le travail, en poésie, est tout! They fought and killed each other many times, while Eve brought forth more children in sorrow, and Adam, his body aching, tilled the land.

Once I taught polar bears to write poetry. After class each week (it was once a week) I came home to bed. The work was extremely tiring. The bears tried to maul me and for months refused to write a single word. If refused is the right term to use for creatures who had no idea what I was doing and what I wanted them to do. One day, however, it was in early April, when the snow had begun to melt and the cities were full of bright visions on windowglass, the bears grew quieter and I believed that I had begun to get through to them. One female bear came up to me and placed her left paw on top of my head. Her mouth was open and her very red tongue was hanging out. I realized that she, and the other bears, must be thirsty, so I procured for them several barrels of water. They drank thirstily and looked up at me from time to time gratefully but even then they wrote no poems. They never did write a word. Still I don't think this teaching was a waste of time, and I'm planning on continuing it in the future if I find I have the necessary strength. For hard and exhausting it is to attempt something one knows it is impossible to do—but what if one day these bears actually started to write? I think we would all put down our Stefan George and our Yeats and pay attention! What wonders might be disclosed! what dreams of bears!

Reading is done in the immediate past, writing in the immediate future.

The world never tires of bad poetry, and for this reason we have come to this garden, which is in another world.

I don't think one can avoid irrationality when one is young if one is planning to enjoy it when one is old. For this reason a poet's life may be called "precarious."

Similarity of sound is similarity of adventure. If you believe that, you are a musician.

Poetry, which is written while no one is looking, is meant to be looked at for all time.

Ballade

EN L'AN SOIXANTE-ONZIEME DE MON AGE

We who have ten years to live, approximately,
Are having a good talk at this party.
Ten years of good health, if we're lucky—
O foot on the moving stair!

EN L'AN QUARANTE-HUITIEME DE MON AGE

Whoever wants to make love to all of them
Women I mean—whoever wants to see all the shows—
Flower, dramas, dog—come forward now
And eat this cheese and see if it will make you want more.

EN L'AN CINQUIEME DE MON AGE

It's okay, pillaging
And loving mud. Knowing my tranquility
Is hard due to constant desire
For education, I steam through a winter's young fires.

EN L'AN QUINZIEME DE MON AGE

Girl with ruffles in your hair
And tussles in your dress
And flamingos for bouche
And gladiolas for clasps gosh we're idiots.

EN L'AN VINGT-DEUXIEME DE MON AGE

I watch this fuel
Burning down
And think I'm an expert
On zooming life.

EN L'AN TRENTE-HUITIEME DE MON AGE

A book comes out. And then another. I'm gratified
Like a house robber. I am planning another side-
Ways book and then another. I go abroad and
Write a play, called "Husband Blubber."

EN L'AN DIX-HUITIEME DE MON AGE

Oh eighteenth year! Truly you are like a jewelry box.
You open and shut with a pam! I know it's over.
Everything is over. The ballgame. My friendship. My romance.
Before my next birthday it seems as though twenty years pass.

EN L'AN SOIXANTE-DEUXIEME DE MON AGE

Lying on the operating table
I wrote a letter to myself in code
And, while the morphine was wearing off,
I had a strange vision of Goldilocks.

EN L'AN SOIXANTE-QUATRIEME DE MON AGE

I lost you, flowers. I lost you, lovely V,
Neckline of straw and flowers, I lost your key. I lost my key.
It could have been everything that I lost
If I had died this year.

EN L'AN SOIXANTE-TREIZIEME DE MON AGE

I am polite to women and puppies
And cross with cads. I have a lot of years and decades in me
And they divide me like Sunday ads.
It's the Big Sale of the Week, when I can speak in song.

EN L'AN ONZIEME DE MON AGE

Occurring and curving and curving and occurring
The dynamic street on which I live
Is blending graciously this evening with another street
On which two whom I play football with live.

EN L'AN QUATORZIEME DE MON AGE

I much prefer the arrondissement
To this terrible year.
My dog becomes hysterical.
I come home to opened doors.

EN L'AN TRENTE-SIXIEME DE MON AGE

My daughter is five years old.
Can you imagine, five?
For five years she has been growing
She has been roving, she has been improving, she has been alive.

EN L'AN VINGT-HUITIEME DE MON AGE

Give me some more poetry and I'll get you some more whiskey
I can drink all night and I can sleep well all morning
I am typing out more poems than there are paintings by Wassily Kandinsky
And, as you know, that's quite a lot.

EN L'AN SIXIEME DE MON AGE

If I pause on my way past the statue of Abraham Lincoln
That sits in front of our school
It is to easily pick up a snowball
And when I throw it to try to nick you on the ear.

EN L'AN CINQUANTE-SEPTIEME DE MON AGE

The worst things that happened
Did not happen before
But happen this year
Like the crack of a gun.

EN L'AN TRENTIESME DE MON AGE

I'm writing like François Villon but not really.
There's no doom in it. I'm not being tried for my life.
I have a thousand years in which to write
A wonderful seamlessness has just come up in my poetry.

Artificial Intelligence

GETTING BACK ON LAND

The arms of those armchairs resemble the legs
Of young women who have just come over
From the coast of America in a tramp steamer;
They sing happily of the long days of their voyage
And they are glad to see the armchairs again, which remind them of their legs.

VIDA BREVE

Nothing else matters, only the clam with the little william nose
And the clive bracelet, and the george scene and the tom acorn;
Here, eat him, now here, eat him; and then smile.

WAHEGO

Aren't you afraid of being a few
Paces behind the Lead Runner
When he reaches the Last Place of Rest?

FROTH

Coppers in the ocean, millions of them, dropped there
By tourists, men and women, who believed
They could do it and make a wish
To be Red masters.

PASSAGE

A boat comes by, captain smiling, lady on his arm
Tatooed there by Plush the Pirate; I wish I were here with you
Written on the paper beneath his pen. Boat goes by with a frown.

MATTERS

At eight o'clock the torn apron was willing
To depart with her lover, the cleaning;
But at the stroke of nine exactly
He was already tired of her and had gone to the hearing
Of sunshine and beautiful ways.

FRAGMENT

Moon in the mirror, are you the same as the one outside
Or are you a different moon, filled with artifice and pride?
Are you like that lady, who . . .

CHIAROSCURO

Other Romes, other moons, other umbrellas.
And streetcleaners, patching up the Forum,
Gaze at us with another sense of space.

THE FLOWERS OF EVIL

Lay on the table
I picked it up
As well as I was able
And grappled with an eagle
Who is my Savior.
Savior mine,
Let me read this book,
I said.
OK said he,
And I read it
While he flew around.
My brain is burning
O eagle, I cried.
Do not fear
I shall be at your side
To quiet your yearning
My Savior replied.

An anthology of Magical poetry
Lay on the table in the rookery
I opened it and began to charm
Began to charm the birds away:

"Robin redbreast and sparrow
Bluefinch of waist that is narrow
Joyous kingfisher, catbird so black
All fly away, and never come back!"

Then from the nuttery
Came a voice so softly
That I could scarcely hear it.
So I drew near it.

It said, "Scaly fish,
Porcupines who never adorn my dish,
Finned carp, and nasal porpoise
Abandon pour toujours my habeas corpus!"

LA DIMINUZIONE DALLA MAMMA

La mia mamma
Nel tempo in cui ero bambino
Fu una donna
Molto grande e molto bella
Allora che ora
E minuscola
Come una cosa
Che si vedrebbe dalla finestra
Di un palazzo, verso la sera,
Come di quest'altezza
Potrebbe sembrare un dente
Di una sconosciuta
Nell'aria bruna di Firenze.

SOLEMN

Les jeunes gens jouent des Checkers
Pendant que leurs grandpapas regardent—d'assez loin.
Their grandfathers are in Mexico City;
One of them is dead, and the other lies very ill
In the Clinica de Los Altos Man.
The boy stares at his checkers, and the other cries "Move!"

FRAGMENT

They wandered in the scorched and gloomy summer
As far as Franklin's beach. Tod stood amazed
At all the huts which dotted now the water.
"Why there is a development here," he muttered,
"Where there before was only beach and sky!"
A large bird fluttered over them, which caught
The first rays of the setting sun, grew pink,
And vanished. Tod took Ellen's hand and smiled:
"So like the bird, so like our good old beach,"
He said . . .

MORRO ROCK

No more sandals made from fibrous particles of lunch
Dropped on the equally fibrous cheerleader. Uhuh, Henry Hudson!

SCHWEITZERREICH

Geneva. A bird call. Someone's name.
Geneva. The flowers. The flower. The Geneva.

VAGABONDS

Vagabonds! that's what we are—vagabonds!
Early in the morning we pack up and change our clothes
Into little strips of cloud
And march forth into the blue universe.
While lingering pennies chime in black pools
We lunch on paralyzing blood-slugs
And drink hog-water.
We are happy at centrifugal force.
We would fly away if we did not like earth so much;
We roll in dung like a scarf of good cheer.

Sometimes meadows consisting wholly of stones
Offer us couches for our revolting amours;
But then, at other times, at the beginning of evening
We stand and watch, enchanted, some human fiesta.

MATEEYANAH

Not like a child but like a wild blackbird
She descended the stairs from her tree.

OFFER

Morning may find us whiter, perhaps surprised
By the clanging streetcar.

NINETEEN THIRTY SIX

Paint the house, painter!
Hit the sidewalk, cement!

LITTLE-KNOWN HISTORICAL FACT

Charlemagne, don't be so unhappy! You gadabout, rain!
The old French king kept sitting sideways
On top of his throne; then he fell off.
"It's raining," said Charlemagne. "Look! La pioggia!"
Charlemagne was an Italian.

THE RUE QUENTIN-BAUCHART IN 1951

It was horsemeat!
Yes, I did.
Did you like it?
Thanks for the lunch.
Okay.
Okay?
No, I have to be going.
Would you like something else?
Did you?
No I else.
Good-bye.

TRIESTE E UNA DONNA

Vagabond silence, music of my tears,
And the whole world of yesterday
Chugging like a train, into Trieste.

GREAT BEAUTY

It's like being received in the arms of a great beauty
When she throws aside her cloak and has nothing on underneath
Except that being received in the arms of a great beauty is better
But I love this fog.

Commosso

Perhaps at the end of the mountains that isn't a woman
But a literary place with tables
Where one can be with friends. But Milan is angry
It is throwing out these terrifying bolts of storm
That sound like a dog who is coming from a far-off country
To meet the master he is going to bite before anything happens
To separate these two and keep them apart
When the storm is over and, settling down again,
Milan seems merely helpful, a source of cash and tourists
Or else annoying, ruining with cash and tourists
Everything it touches and that touches it but not this storm
That shows the end of the mountains where lie love,
Friendship, and work, if only I can find them
With the help of these extravagant flashes and the rain
That spends its wild excitement on the water.

The True Story of the Mule

Enjoying everyone
It meets
Like a sunrise
Over distant facades.

Ulla

I followed the young woman—Ulla, was that her name?
Down the hallway—what a strange destiny it is
To be so beautiful! I followed
And that was all I was doing—following. It was not a Civil War
Thank goodness! not even something I had to work on
And as some would follow a matador and others a thrilling soprano
I walked on after this Ulla down the hall
To a light and airy room. She said, This is your chamber.
You will stay here tonight, and, then, tomorrow morning
We will change you to another one, which is a little bit more comfortable
    than this.
I'm perfectly happy with this room, I said. I thought,
Today I've seen Ulla. Is that enough? But, well,
Yes, now, could you show me the other
Where tomorrow I may be lodging. The rooms are national.
Ulla is one part of what is real. She says, yes,
Please follow me. On the walls are designs of roses and of fleurs-de-lys.

The Promenade of the Ghostly Subtitles

It was the time of the promenade of the ghostly subtitles
No one could prevent their walking forth
Everywhere you looked you would see *A Girl's Story* or
Vignettes of the Andalusian Forest or something of that sort,
While the real titles, slumbering in ignorance of this,
The great, heavy, burdensome, entitled titles,
The big, even gigantic refreshing and obvious titles,
The gorgeous titles, the fine titles, the magnificent ones,
Home for the Holidays, Anna Karenina, War and Peace, David Copperfield,
The Red and the Black, Father Goriot, Barchester Towers, Emma, Hamlet,
    Julius Caesar, Death on the Installment Plan, Wozzeck,
Lay dead to the world in castles, chateaus and villas
All round the earth, while the subtitles sauntered forth
As if they were titles, showing the world their value
Which once the titles awoke they would never have.

The Seasons

To James Thomson

I *Spring*

Now pizza units open up, and froth
Steams forth on beers in many a frolic bar
New-opened-up by April. People find
White sheets and envelopes that blow through streets
And pick them up to read them but to find
That it is SPRING and all is vain to read.
Lovers, of course, avuncular old men,
And primrose-cheeked domestics pushing strollers
Meet smiling then pursue their golden ways
Down sunlight-sparkled vales of plain cement.
The red transforms to green. 'Tis silence all,
And pleasing expectation. Herds and flocks
Drop the dry sprig, and mute-imploring eye
The falling verdure. Boys and girls exclaim
In wonder at the new-arriving tides
Of energy's full swell. Up springs the bark
Of Peppy who's been left, tied by a string
Of stout white cord to a tough lamppost gnarled
With many a dolloped spackle of green paint
Implanted in the sidewalk like an oak
That outward further spreads its soft regret
That it is not spring always. To such post
Is Peppy tied while that into the shop
For a new lacy bra his mistress bides
And looks at stockings also. Peppy's yell
Is springtime's herald, all its mighty morn
Is welcomed by his yapping; and some birds
On nearby roofs take up his rough exclaim
And parcel it in sweets of various kinds.
What passing fellow with his shirt undone
One or two buttons down a whistle on
His lips looks round and pities Peppy there
But does not when he sees that beauty leave
The shop door open half behind and dog

Now straining at what improvised as leash
Could much serve to un-breath him did not she,
One package under her left arm, another
Tucked in with it, release him from the post
And let him jump upon her like the leaves
That West Wind blows in autumn's coming days.
Flushed by the spirit of the genial year
And by the smile of Bob who at her side
Now asks her if some package he can take
To make her task the easier, she says yes,
For she has need of help, the knot once tied
So quickly now resists but with two hands
Free for this enterprise she does it well.
Thank you she says and asks her bundles back.
Bob, teasing won't return them, then he does.
She smiles, relieved. He dares and asks her out
What of some coffee in O'Toole's Garage
The place right on the corner there? Okay!
Do they let dogs in? Yes I think they do
And Peppy jumps, to emphasize his thought
That where Louise goes he goes with her now
And would not stay imprisoned any more
To yap at the green budding all around.
This once agreed, the two walk slowly down
The emerald-studded street, green lights on green.
Bob's feet feel easy moving in their shoes
And on the virgin's cheek a fresher bloom
Than ever was before is now perceived.
Her lips blush deeper sweets; she breathes of youth;
The shining moisture swells into her eyes
In brighter flow; her wishing bosom heaves
With palpitations wild; kind tumults seize
Her veins, and all her yielding soul is love.
Bob doesn't know this as he chats away
Telling this girl of his accomplishments
In selling carburetors which she loves
To hear about because that magic tinge
Of fresh beginning that was clear just now
In Peppy's bark roves scintillant in her.
What kinds of carburetors, used or new?
She asks him and he takes her trembling hand
To lead her, Peppy held by t'other one,

His leash, into the midst of the Garage
A fashionable place to sit this spring
And drink non-alcoholic drinks and say
Inane things to your loved one while the light
Comes smashing through the glass in images
That never are forgotten being those
Associate with such dear starts of love.
Now Peppy barks, and barks. The waitress says
He'll have to go outside. So all three leave
Go somewhere else and never do find out
Why Peppy barked. Enough to say perhaps
He's worried for Louise. "Ah, then, ye fair,
Be greatly cautious of your sliding hearts,"
Perhaps he barked, not saying, for even spring
Cannot give power of words to canine kind,
And barking so may have felt the frustration
All lesser creatures feel when close to us
Yet taking in our power, energy
Which once they've felt they scarce can live without;
So we perhaps with spring are in this state.
In any case, Louise now bares her arm
To look at a small smutch on it was made
By Peppy's jump and Bob's heart skips two beats.
Rattled he laughs. She smiles. Now in the Park
Where woodbines flaunt and roses shed a couch
Peppy lies down, and our two humans sit
And contemplate the splendor of the season
Though scarce aware of other things. Bob says,
"Louise, now pepper plants begin to leaf
And, next, to bud, beside the canopy
O'erhanging Mrs. Olson's Fudge Bazar—
I'd like to walk you someday on that street
And" then he smiled and then he turned away
He'd seen a robin fluttering in retreat
From a crouched cat who stood the oak beside
To which the bird had fluttered. Peppy, tense
At visioning the feline, strained his leash
Till it was almost bursting. With a tug
Bob pulls him back and with the pup in tow
And Robin Redbreast safe within his tree,
Resumes—"And oh so many other places,
There are so many places we can go

While April spackles sap in every smudgeon
And banner of surcease." He glanced around
Then pulled the young girl to him without sound,
Her blue-blouse-clad back clasped his hands around
And felt like his her heart begin to pound.
He kissed her. At that moment Peppy dulled
For a few moments by the episode
That separates him from the cat and bird
Now leaps again to life and yaps aloud
At what is happening to his mistress. Harm?
No harm yet, Peppy: she is happily
Embraced by one she finds good all around.
And Peppy quiets. Then there is no sound
Save for the gentle murmurs made by love
When two draw back from kiss and gaze around
Amazed at where they are and what they've found.
Leaves, even as they sit there, come to shape
On many a slender branch; and, low, the worm
Inventive, cramps for space in paths well hidden
From yellow-shaded beak with tints of rose
In clacking quest for quell of appetite.
Now Bob stands up, he gives Louise his hand
And bids her to observe the vernal scene
Before they amble further. "Fairest One!
Look! Thespius ropes Coniglia with his bars
And Leonine protects the rule of three.
New shirts are worn, no stockings, and new shoes
New blouses blossom. Air creeps past its post
And stations coolness on a breast or thigh
That hitherto was covered or if numb
From other gesture not so simply spanned.
Long legs are looming past, and biscuits dance
In popping ovens for the furious taste
Of casual strollers in the urban glare
Of April sunlight like an opened cave
In which the diamonds of Hesperides
Are cast in all their gleaming. To decide
To not walk thither on a day like this
Is to be pent in prison like a rug
Rolled up and in the warehouse. Let us drive
Or walk or leap with such impulsive aim
That we bounce high on this day's trampoline!"

II *Summer*

So do they prosper, and so do we look
To the next season now, whose mighty sun
Unbolts the doors and steams the swimming pools.
From brightening fields of ether fair disclosed
Child of the Sun, refulgent SUMMER comes
Colossal with its shining envelope
Of white hydrangeas flush to nature's green
Defenses unencumbered. Roses mount
Erupt in fragrant blossom pinkest white
And reddish hue and then are seen no more
Till early autumn taps them with a spout
Of latter-springing laughter. Lavender,
Sansevieria, scabiosa prim
As other evening light in bloodied mode
And portulaca hovering next to him,
Godetia grandiflora, morning glory,
Ajuga, azeratum, columbine—
All these and more come crowding, none to stay
Yet powered each with the capacity
To flower and stay flowered if but for
What moments they enchant us. Rabbits bound
Less than they did in spring but still there are
Enough to fill the gardens with the bites
Unauthorized that bring the gardener down
To knees to note his basil and his thyme
In an imperfect state, which have been bit
By some young rodent's teeth who then away
Into the meadows lush with clover leaps
Then burrows in the ground, where it is cool
Within the bosom of the panting earth—
Hot outside, inside cool, creative earth!
That, by the summer mothered, gestures forth
Such produce as imprinted on our tongues
Descends into our muscles, skin, and bones
And redesigns our essence, in accord
With that First Contract by which growing things
Give nurture to us that we here remain
In body and in soul to see once more

The seasons' lazy susan whirl around.
And what in country brings the flower and fruit
In town brings on the people. End of dark—
Roused by the clock, the quick-clad city youth
Leaves the apartment-fold in which he dwells
To journey through the summer-morning-sweet
Unending avenues that Gotham gives
To those who wake in summer soon and glad.
Till when arrived at office where the sun
Blinds through the windows harming not with heat
As insulation and conditioned air
Make their own spring of summer, he may smile
At rosy-fingered thoughts, that on his desk
The contract for a Coliseum lies
That will transform him to a billionaire.
Be quiet, quiet my heart! He breathes and stands
A moment with heart shaking. Then he tends
Slow, downward, to his chair. Is it too much
To hope of summer morning that one be
Transformed to such a person? It may be
Only a dream that lingered in his thoughts
That waking should have transferred. He's a clerk
And has more modest duties to perform
Than those that populate his fantasies.
And fifty floors below him the young bum
Who long has taken alcohol for wife
Stands in a daze, one hand extended. But
A grey-garbed kindly Quaker woman there
Gives him the hand of friendship, not a coin,
And may convince him, in the dulcet air
Of summer morn to try to take a cure.
And it is so. He follows her. Good luck!
Though hard it is to give addiction up,
It's kindness and concern that give best chance
Not prison and dour drubbing. On this block
Performs the hot dog man his ritual task
Of feeding those who wander through the streets,
Or haste, they run, for they'll be late for jobs
And had not time to pour the foamy cream
Into their blazing coffee. No, they leapt
Almost unclothed outside and ran to catch
The seven-twenty or six-forty-five

To way downtown Manhattan then to run
To their old building but can scarce resist
The summer fragrance of the hot dog stand.
Here hot dogs sizzle at the curb, there flash
From windows rays of sunlight that bedazzle
The eyes of those who buy them and begin
To take a bite before the change is given
For the five dollar bill they have extended
To the frankfurter salesman, smiling man
In workaday blue apron with two hands
That rapidly can shuffle sauerkraut
Between two halves of bun and with his spoon
Or ladle slap the mustard on, present
The finished hot dogs to the waiting friends
Ere they were conscious he had yet begun.
So they begin to nibble, to resist
Is vain, for the aroma brings them in
And heat to heat doth drive the splanging tongue
To ever more endeavour through the kraut
And then, cold Doctor Pepper there beside
Clamped in one's other hand, one takes a swallow
And feels emparadised, with golden birds
Incumbent of their wingspans all around.
Yet pent-up in the city in the worst
Of suffocating summer, Man take care!
Or else survive not to the season's end!
For these bright times can sudden darkness bring—
Heart surgeons reap a harvest: people drop
In doorways and on driveways, stop in cars
And never start again, run to the pump
But do not reach it, fail to find the way
To serve the tennis ball but find instead
They are face-down on the court. Unhappy game!
It may be Jane who grieves for Albert then
His lifetime ended by a strike of sun.
But no, now he recovers and stands up
Though weak and dazed, his hand upon the net—
Oh they will stop to drink in swift delight
Some haughty iced tea of the afternoon
And till Al's heartbeat's normal once again
Not stir one inch from such beatitude
As death makes known when breath to life returns.

Many, when city streets become so hot
As to resemble radiated halls
And every moment's like some blanket that
Comes stifling down to make the chance to breathe
Unusual without a choke of pain,
Look at the weather and decide it's wise
To pack the trunks and towels and seek the beach
Where Oceanus like a freezy coin
Of green-blue gold and silver brings to play
Upon hot legs and faces sprigs of wind
That make the heart a placid occupant
Of the o'erheated body that it was.
Bronzed boys and girls stride slimly down the sands
And dash into the surf as if themselves
They were cool sticks of summer like the trees
That hide themselves in mass of foliagery—
Now these are hid in foam and off they swim
And clash about and touch each other's arms
And shoulders; now hand on a waist is placed
And one drawn to another in a scene
Of mermaid/merman swift frivolity
Unchaperoned by any but the waves.
On shore, they pile up castles in the sand,
Build campfires, and sing songs till the shy moon
Comes plunging upward into the dim sky
Of night when all regain their shady homes.
Some older persons too come to the beach
And 'neath umbrellas watch the thunderous waves,
Admiring youth in what they see and feel
And read, forgetful of the sun-stung streets
They left to voyage here. Or it may be
One falls in love with a brown-shouldered girl
With whom one later may abridge the time
Of being in the sun by seeking shade
Of arm and shoulder or the ascending knee
That brings the leg with it and sometimes all
Of the loved body making a young tent
To give such cool with such solicitude
The whole life breathes with it and is engaged;
So far no such event, but each may dream
In summer of such unprepared elans
That mix the dark and light by varied means.

Too hot, just hot enough, in shade, ablaze—
All those who love such changes and do read
These sun-flocked pages standing near the rock
On which the lichen of distress looks out
Will know a scene of power. For as the bee
Full of his quizzing and his upscale sum
Of sun-delighting symmetries does one
And then another flip-up off to green
From green, so shall one message from the sun
Be weight enough to tip the scales of dreams
And make them in accord with where they beckon
And toward which they resume their silent strains.

III *Autumn*

But now hear AUTUMN bellow from the trees
And send to us the first announcing drops
Of harvest rain. Busses wait at their stops
A little longer in the cooling breeze
As more each day get onto them and off.
Oh time delighting, to be back in school!
Back with the bright cool bodies of the girls
And the bold sturdy bodies of the boys
Who are the same age and who were last year
The same age also but are older grown
And larger and of more connecting heft!
To fly into the classroom like a wave
Of idiot excitement and be quelled
One brief hour only by the teacher's drawl
Who teaches us a little though we find
Truth more gigantic in the sexual mind
That steers us through the corridors with bump
Occasional, deliberate of some one
We wish to hug or battle with, toward lunch
Appalling in the cafeteria dim
Then in the mind proud Mathematics sports
Till once again at three o'clock one finds
The world delicious as a lemon rind
In a martini, serve it to us straight
This tactile joy of autumn, when the skin
Of arbors reddens, flushed with bliss of change.

Now wheat crops come to harvest; blooming late
Chrysanthemums adorn the garden's edge
Autumn affects the gutters; through the streets
A rush of water comes, for it has rained
And rained and rained, I think it rained all night.
And moody earth, true to the prophesies
Of spring and summer shows its treasures forth
Of pumpkins and potatoes, and the proud
Zucchini and the squash and melon huge—
Portentous products whose gay husks conceal
Inside such tastes as to the earth re-wed

Our selves, divorced by being, yet to which,
Less soon than these, yet soon, our husks return.
And, in cemented city, apples shine
In outdoor markets, moist inside bright skins,
All ready to be taken with a smile
And bitten with anticipated twinge
Most redolent of autumn on the tongue.
Bob Blentz comes by and buys one which he bites
As Microsoft goes plunging down which bites
The young investor; nights like summer nights
Yield to some somewhat colder ones, and tents
Are taken down and folded. Ducks and geese
Whizz overhead to Carolinas, quit
Of cooling air which soon into deep freeze
Would place them, not to be revived next year.
And the World Series closes like a fist
On all that has been baseball. One home run
In such a game may justify the life
On one fall day of that autumnal man
Who bats the ball out of the park then runs
With hands extense above his capless dome
Fist clenching and unclenching, in his eyes
Catching the solar dazzle. At his name
Swell baseball-crazy hearts which find in this
Cool season summer pastime's apogee
And thrill to that which now must be forgot
Until next spring, swift fallen like the leaves.
Tuned in, though far from Stadium or Shea,
Miss Lisbeth in her Austin drives along
East Twenty-First Street marvelling at fall
And so does Mr. Peterson the grump
Of Twenty-Ninth and Broadway who ascends
A stairway in his antiquated home
Once the apartment of a billionaire
But now a place divided into ten
Apartments each one smaller than the next
Through which however now an autumn breeze
Blows rapid breaths delighting one and all.
And Hugo now a new apartment finds
For Sarah. They for weeks have scanned the ads
For someplace in a neighborhood she'll like
While autumn dusts the windows with its leaves

And now at last have found one. He believes
It's better for them that they live apart
A while; it's a mistake. But now they smile
At every detail of the place, and light
A fire in the fireplace and, content
For what shall be short time, find in a kiss
What seems an answer even to the pain
Such short-lived bliss must cause. From poultry shelves
Gobblers are grabbed and gutted for the clones
Of passionate pilgrims whom digestion greets
Traditionally on one cold clean day
While cranberries are roughed from swamp and pond
Until one might esteem that cool Cape Cod
Had lost the blush of youth but to grow pale
For pleasures of the feasting multitudes.
Then harmless sweet potatoes, too, are set
Upon the coals to please and warm our jaws;
Amidst the strip-tease oaks and birches here.
Yet still there's time to travel! Fall is kind
To whoso has fond wish to reinvent
This earth's imagined confines. Sweet it is,
Cool-clad in hopes, to take one's wallet out
And buy the tickets that in fair exchange
Get one an airplane seat, which, sinking down
Onto a field near Venice, jolts and bumps
And then grows still, as one goes out to see
This treeless town of autumn at its best,
Where the Casino like an emerald shines
Atop the silver-circling Grand Canal—
Or northward makes its landing: I have stood
In the Place Saint Sulpice and wished to die
I was so full of happiness, one hour
When autumn brushed the stemless stones with gems
Of intellectual brilliance, like desire
For what we have but dare not call our own.
And then return with winter drawing near—
Fall, thou ambiguous season, who begin
With the red cast-off sun-scorched skin of summer
And end with winter's pallor, hear oh hear
My chant to thee, harbinger of rebirth
Of school and love and work, and scene of death
That in thy colors stuns us dim with joy

Till hap we feel the wild cold-warm confusion
Confucius once when rapt in Glade of Ho
Felt stumbling on a rattler and being bid
By conscience to step back, not harm the thing,
But human instinct urging him to fear
Did pound it with a stone—then, quick, aghast,
Through autumn's cool bamboo that halled his home
Turbulent fled and wrote his *Analects*
A source of wisdom for all time to come.
'Tis Autumn brings such changes most, its dark
Mortality that sparks ascending life—
Leaves flushed by color look like cardinals,
And cardinals like energetic leaves—
Together cardinals in red leaves do make
A red embrasure that the wind does shake—
And brings revival where was almost not
The hope of something living—work by dead.
Chagall adorns the Modern, Henry Moore
Is spread out all along Park Avenue;
De Kooning has at last come into focus
For multitudes who, standing in the Met
Before his sitting Women, feel the crazed
Delight of stout Balboa, termed Cortez
By dreamy Keats, when once in Darien
He stared at the Pacific, all alone
In speculation, circled by his men.
All this the human soul absorbent makes
Contiguous to its essence, and looks out
At the confounding city whipped by breeze
And, breathing in what life is breathing there,
Becomes a thing autumnal of its own.

IV *Winter*

If the west wind is Autumn's, what is that
Which WINTER gives to speed the skates along?
To freeze the engine while the snowball fights
Erupt on guttered streets and garbage trucks
Pick up the snow and let the garbage stay
A while in plastic bags for rats to seek
Out every night impenetrable not
To those sharp teeth? Oh, from what Arctic bulge
Of everlasting winter slicked by spring
And summer with its meltingness re-formed
Into another shape as fearsome and
Relentless as its former, does there come
A messenger with one would say a hope
To pry conversion from the temperate zones
Convincing them with killing blasts of air
That sempiternal winter would be best
For everything there living? Spring has marked
The one end of this season as has fall
The other, yet, ignoring these, it comes
As it would stay forever. Flying force,
Go back to that sad cemeteried zone
In which you prosper, being there the king,
Unwanted here where soft erupts the rose,
The pear tree blossoms, and the children walk
To playgrounds through the heaps of autumn leaves,
With warm and cool, to each appointed each
A guardian and a limiting effect
Caught in the mild democracy of days.
Return, return thy spite! And yet it stays,
And while it stays brings railings to which stick
The hands, and chill that makes the limbs to shake
To point of death sometimes although we try
To shelter those who lack the force to place
Warmth's wall between its bristling and their lives.
Unknowing its harsh powers some lucky young
May find it pleasure purely, and indeed
May all who have the means to keep them warm
For in contrast is pleasure—the swift sting
Of wind is bound by a fur-coat embrace
In a light-wingèd mix of joy and pain

And few would banish winter from their midst
Could they quell its excess. Amantha slips
Her formal on that shows her shoulders smooth
And white as all that snow. Warm paradox
Of dressing up in winter to be bare
Beneath the glowering chandeliers of heaven
Two instants to the car! And she goes down
The stairs into her waiting date's hired car
And is whisked off to Princeton for a ball
While gentle flakelets flutter in the sky.
Now bold Arcturus weaves for the event
A sudden dreadful thunder that portends
A storm to bring New Jersey to its knees.
Amantha's scared. But Tom says "Oh there, there!
There's nothing to be scared about, I'm here—"
And puts his hand upon her shoulder, which
Brings both a soft delight." "Oh you are mine."
"Yes, I am yours if we get through this storm,"
Amantha says; and they get through the storm.
Princeton is radiant. Red and dark blue lights
Shine through the sleepless snow that hides each ledge
And every dancer feels upon his head
A little of that wildness and that cold.
This leads to some lovemaking in the cars
And to long mornings after spent in bed
With pleasant hangovers and gilded arms
From sunlight that comes through the frosted pane.
There on the pillow rests the golden head
Of captivant Amantha whom beside
Restless the cat of Tom sends forth in glee
His tiny claws to test the mattress out
And tears the sheet a little. Oh that's nothing!
Cries Tom who, just awaked from a sweet dream
Of carnivals' inflexible parades
With snow explosions scared by colored lights,
Can only smile at everything there is
Within him and around him. "Fair Amanth!"
He calls the girl, and she to him replies
"Inevitable Tom, my winter's love!"
Then out again, but careful! Tom descries
Pure purple winter lunging through the skies
And whistles to Amantha, "Let's go home!"

This boreal light has angels of its own
That in no milder season hearts can find.

So some being hastened to a matinee
Of *L'Elisir d'Amore* ride through snow
On taxi's spattering rims to hear the soul
Of Pavarotti melted into song
Swirling among the shoulders bare and proud
Of radiant women who are gathered here
To see the opera and be seen themselves
As lovelier still—but cannot be to those
Like Bob and Humphrey standing at the bar
Poor standees stand at to await the thrill
Of some high tone globescent with the heat
Of universal energy, at which
To cheer, ev'n weep, as if that note were home,
Unknown, unseen, for many a forlorn year
And now made present through a door of song!
Or NORMA sings, or TOSCA, and in waves
Of bright effluent heat comes the applause
Of all who here from brittlest winter's day
Have sought a costly refuge. Wreathed in furs,
Others find naught so bracing as a zoo.
These fanciers most delight in the white bears
Who name the polar region as their home,
Which beasts give courage to the urban throng
Who see them lope, with fascinated eye,
From one height to another in their pen
Constructed to resemble something like
A cold place they might live in but do not.

And, see great trains run like demented creatures
From one place to another finding stations
To house them on their way! Enormous things
Like bridges aqueducts and factories sting
The brittle air with sharpness like its own.
And by the frost refined the whiter snow
Is crusted hard and sounding to the tread
Of early salesman as he nervous seeks
His office door, hopes for a killing, but
So taken with that unanimity
Of white all but forgets his chance and walks

This way and that to see the little caves
And craters deep created by his tread.
Elsewhere the snowplow wanders, with its task
Of clearing ways where stocked with antifreeze
Much frailer vehicles may journey take.
Here Celia's father mystified by storm
That piles a sum of snow before him on
The road now blocked impossible, with joy
And tense relief, a plow's proboscal heave
Considers, grateful for its aptitudes.
The plow has many errands, many streets
And lawns and driveways and industrial parks
And fairgrounds swift with lights in summer now
Bedredged with blue of snowglow, which it owes
And must incite to clearance on this day.
Don Muff the snowplow driver heaves a ton
Of white from place to place and would be known
As a great sculptor if the thing were done
With an aesthete's attention but is not
Alas yet glad the rows of random piles
Do make the hearts of Alex and Cecile
Who sidle mittened through it, giving yells
To show each other which they roam behind.

And then what pleasure when first hint appears
That Winter's reign is over! It had seemed
It would be cold forever but not so.
Friends come with frost upon their cuffs but smiles
Upon their faces that betoken some
Small mutual understanding with the time
That all may soon be well. It's March the first
And we can't tell each morning if we should
Dress for the cold or not. Today we will,
For Boreas only coughs, not dying gasps.
Yet days grow longer and the chilled romance
Of lipstick-smearing seeming endless nights
Veered to the side lies haplessly enditched
Encroached upon by crocus. And how strange
That Winter will be battered down by Spring,
Which like a babe on Goliathic rocks
Melts them with his attentions, kissing stone
And turning it to roseleaf, basil, sun.

He takes the Old Man's house, his hearth, his wife
And finally deprives him of his being,
This childlike innocent who seemed a son
Of gentler nature but whose bite is stronger
Than winter's teeth e'er muster, ending knocked
Across the way by primaveral fist.
But yet not yet—still, with the bitter wind,
A gasp of dying that is no less fierce
Than at its midmost raving cuts the tape
Of morning to let peep the frozen day.

Sing louder, bird hibernal, if you please!
I shall not quail at your more vatic strains
But be content to have perceived so far
Into the whites of these four seasons' eyes,
Perceived young lovers in them touched by sun
Or in the snow in parks and on the roads
And to have known the anguish and the change
Of bitter disparition and the bite
Of what seems not to come but then perhaps
Does come, or then does not, or not renews,
And to have felt the blood in changing flow
That seasons bring, and the light grace of flesh
In cold or warmer weather, to have known
The change that does not change, in being change
Itself, the clime in which we most must run
And so find Thomson's reasons and our own
To go on living at their latitudes
And in the range of how they most appear.

SONGS FROM THE PLAYS

"Around the hero, everything becomes a tragedy.
Around God, everything becomes what? a world?" NIETZSCHE

"Around songs, everything becomes a play." SHAKESPEARE

Bring back the beds

Bring back the beds
And the hotels
And the sheets
All the pillows
Red of flowers
Out the windows
In a contract
An option
To do
Again what we
Did do
How often?
Make love
—Two hundred times?

Summer Vacation

Let the obi fall

Let the obi fall
Energy is all
Don Juan of Kyoto!

Women of the night
Standing left and right
Don Juan of Kyoto!

Peace is a ball
That rolls through space
And holds up time

With energy!
Obi! Obi!
Let it fall!

Don Juan of Kyoto

This dancing man was once the Pope

This dancing man was once the Pope
The leader of all Christians
His dancing partner, she
Was President of Israel.
These others, gathered round,
Were nothing quite so grand.
"Pius!" they cry, "With Golda
Please dance another round!"
He is a dancing man
And she a dancing woman. That is all
We know of them
And all we need to know.

Easter in the Vatican

When I was a young woman

When I was a young woman
Before I came to Israel
I never dreamed that I
Would spread beneath the sky
Patriotic motions
Patriotic notions
Patriot emotions
Country-serving words!

It is hot in Haifa
And it is hot in Tel Aviv
I would be a dancer
Before my senses leave
My mortal, grand persona
And either go to sleep
Or join some other soldier
Some other mighty Golda! Oh I weep
That it may chance again!

Easter in the Vatican

Your genius made me shiver
It seemed to me
That you were greater than I
Could ever be
Your genius made me shiver.

Pure genius makes us shiver
We who want to be
Torn out of history
And raised up to be
Intellectual heroes.

How easily you do
What I must work to do
Long and long hours
How quickly you renew
Your much-spent powers.

Your genius makes to shiver
All those who have forever
Longed, longed for the caress
Of glory and the Muses
Who, all, know now that they shall have it less

Than you shall have it, ever—
Illumined, and onrushing like a river.

Brothers and Friends

Let us praise the elephant

Let us praise the elephant
Oooh hooo bando!
The elephant is severe and great
Ohh hah bando lai go shi
Manageable elephant
Hoo tai yan!
Unmanageable tree—
O bajyo!
He will tear it down
We will make a town—
Ban do he mai ho shi!
A town of broken branches
Wooden city!
The elephant brings it down—
Man gai no chi!

Under the Savanna's Blue Sky

Africa paese notturno

Africa paese notturno
You turn out the light
And we are in Africa
Africa the country of night
Africa the city of night
Africa the village of night
Africa my Africa

But, ah! turn it back on
And Africa is gone!
In the lights of the coming dawn
And in the haze of noon
Africa paese diurno—
One continent gone, one returns
With one ray of light
Africa my Africa

Under the Savanna's Blue Sky

How in her pirogue she glides

How in her pirogue she glides
Like a flower seen from all sides!
She the universe divides
Into sunshine, rain, and snow.

Wonder when she will decide
To get out and from which side
Then all eyes shall she divide
By the way she means to go

But not yet. Like lily still
Upon the Congo's moving hill
She floats, and makes men's hearts to ride,
Like boats, themselves, upon the running tide.

Edward and Christine

Driving along

Driving along
His pregnant wife is in
The other seat the
Baby sings a song:
"I want to be born" etc.
"I want to be born" etc.
"I want to be born" etc.
"Tonight"
"Unto this planet."

New Faces of Forty Years Past

Mediterranean suns

Mediterranean suns!
Shine on, in, and around
To light up our sterns and our prows
And to keep us out of trouble
By showing us the waves
That loop around our boat!
It's made of wood
And linen. Come down
From Antibes, come down
From Nice, from Cannes
Come down into my boat.
The Mediterranean sun
Is shining on the boat.
Won't you come, too,
From the fresh air
Of these resorts?
Just climb down.

New Faces of Forty Years Past

They say Prince Hamlet's found a Southern island

They say Prince Hamlet's found a Southern island
Where he lies happy on the baking sand
A lovely girl beside him and his hand
Upon her waist and is completely silent;
When interviewed, he sighs, and makes a grand
Gesture toward the troubled Northern places.
I know them not, he cries, and love them less.
Then he is once more lost in loveliness.

They say King Lear, recovered in his mind
From all those horrors, teaches now at some
Great university. His course—*Cordelia*—
Has students by the thousands every term.
At course's end, he takes his students out,
Points to the clouds and says You see, you see her!
And every one, unable not to cry,
Cries and agrees with him, and he is solaced.

O King, you should retire and drink your beer!
And Hamlet you should leave your happy island
And wear, with fair Ophelia, Denmark's crown.

Shakespeare Amended

Why should Denmark grip my mind

Why should Denmark grip my mind
When all delights upon this shore I find?
Denmark with its freezing rain
And my father's dying pain
My false mother and her lover—
No, all that, is over, over!
Blue transparence of this sky
Where it would even be sweet to die
Upon the midnight without caring
Merged with love and all love's daring
Breasts lips eyes legs arms and belly
Turning senses into jelly
Why go back to Denmark's numbing
Sleets and snows? Say I'm not coming!
Poor Ophelia's dead and buried.
Sweet Belinda, we are married
By the breeze the sand the foam—
They shall be our hecatomb.

Shakespeare Amended

If I am to be preserved from heartache and shyness

If I am to be preserved from heartache and shyness
By Saint Catherine of Siena,
I am praying to her that she will hear my prayer
And treat me in every way with kindness.

I went to Siena to Saint Catherine's own church
(It is impossible to deny this)
To pray to her to cure me of my heartache and shyness
Which she can do, because she is a great saint.

Saint Catherine of Siena, if this song pleases you,
Then be good enough to answer the prayer it contains.
Make the person that sings this song less shy than that person is,
And give that person some joy in that person's heart.

Masters of the Sun and Sea

Songs are about death

Songs are about death
And life is about stopping
For a while.
Time is about death
And space is about stopping
For a while.
Thought is about death
And sight is about stopping
For a while.

The Unicorn

Allegheny menaces

Allegheny menaces
But B and O declares
We are very happy people
With our Railroad Shares!

Bought at half a dollar
Mounted now to ten
We shall soon be able to
Go back to Gottingen again

And see the varied flowers
Green and white and blue
And walk about the German streets
As the rich people do!

Tuskegee is flighty
Western is a gem
Buy them right and sell them right
And we'll go home again!

New Times, New World

This life which seems so fair

This life which seems so fair
Is like a bubble blown up in the air
By sporting children's breath
Who chase it everywhere
And life is like a market
Open at six A.M.
To which nobody comes
They don't know it's a market
And life is like a gun
Carried in someone's pocket
It shoots the bubbles from the air
And closes down the market.

New Times, New World

Lo where Haussmann comes, see where he comes

Lo where Haussmann comes, see where he comes
To put these projects into execution!
What is that sound I hear? the sound of drums?
No it is Haussmann and the execution
Of his great project, tearing up the streets
Which, as we witness, he completes—
To widen the Champs Elysées
And Paris make, in every way,
The equal of Imperial Rome—
See him, now where he comes!
To shuffle little streets like cards
And deal them out as boulevards,
Avenues shining straight and wide
With a park on every side,
Brilliant streets that radiate
At a white and lovely rate
To Denfert or Passy slim as a bar!
Woods at Boulogne and Vincennes
And at Buttes-Chaumont for workingmen—
Oh, see where Haussmann comes, see where he comes!

Angelica, or Paris in the Nineteenth Century

The Banquet Song

Ah, sweet Banquet, lovely Banquet
From your seats you get your name
From the bench, banchetto, banquette
But from love you get your fame
Love and drink and song and friendship
We extol you from our benches!

Banquet, Banquet, holy Banquet
Here the spirit is transcendent
Joined by wine and wit and laughter
No one soul is independent
All are joined in one enormous
Vision of the life before us!

Ah sweet Banquet thank you thank you
Banquet hear our glasses ring
We shall do our best to make you
A fiesta'd everything!
Such a Banquet as has never
Been and which will last forever!

The Banquet

Let's pour Coca Cola on the Priest

Let's pour
Coca Cola
On the Priest
While he's asleep!

This day is long
The cherries blossom
Life is strong
And he's asleep!

Each temple garden
Awakes from sleep
The sand is strong
In shining mist.

Let's go, pour
Coca Cola on
The Priest
While he's asleep!

Don Juan of Kyoto

I am Death I'll take the hand

I am Death I'll take the hand
Of Borodin the baker
Alfred Schmitz the organ maker
And Jolie la Villette, the sailors' friend.
You turn away. Oh come and dance
The dance is life, and all your life,
And you had better know—
O doctor, O professor,
Young fop or fashion model, where you go
Is where my will directs
To that place where there is no sex
Nor any sport nor holding court
Nor bright ship sailing into port
For each is there alone.

Summer Vacation

Does the sun use you

Does the sun use you
Dead friend
To re-charge its light?
Do those waves
Out there
Have the curls of your hair?
Did you give back to the skies
The deep blue of your eyes?
Has your wit, your wonderful conversation
Become a science in other minds?

Summer Vacation

In Ancient Times

In Ancient Times
The Swedish coast was like a desert place
Snow blossomed, and the surf.

We had a King,
A Senate, and a City,
Several cities, everything.

Everything, but not
What that near Future brought,
Inspired Oxen!

Peace they gave us and
The Great
Society of Love! They gave us Love!

Happy the Swedish nation
All her days
Happy sensation
Oxen children everywhere
We will become the most beautiful
People on earth
Especially our women
Beautiful from loving oxen
What truly are oxen
But men of great worth
Transformed to four-legg'd creatures
With bestial naive features
But these are changed by love!
Oh this is a time of triumph
And a time for celebration
The oxen came to Sweden
They guide us to the future
To future love!
The oxen bring us power and bring us love!

The Strangers from the Sea

The true life

"The true life
Is the life of the ancestors
And the true village
Is the village under the ground."

Come with me to this village!
Beginning to go under the ground
We see the new life
Of seeds sprouting

"Come with us up from the ground
To the village of breathable air!"

Under the Savanna's Blue Sky

Might I be the first

Might I be the first
I would not be worst
I should have the chance
To make my country dance
Yet if I should fail
How my face would pale!
I will risk it all
Bless me, heaven's ball,
All revealing sun,
But tell not my fears to anyone.

We must make raids, raids, raids,
Raids on the English supplies!
Raids in the morning
And raids at night,
Raids in the evening, by candle light
We must make raids!

Raids for clothing
And raids for food
To do the Revolutionary
Army good!
We must make raids
Raids! raids!
Oh raids on the English supplies!

George Washington Crossing the Delaware

You want a social life, with friends

You want a social life, with friends,
A passionate love life and as well
To work hard every day. What's true
Is of these three you may have two
And two can pay you dividends
But never may have three.

There isn't time enough, my friends—
Though dawn begins, yet midnight ends—
To find the time to have love, work, and friends.
Michelangelo had feeling
For Vittoria and the Ceiling
But did he go to parties at day's end?

Homer nightly went to banquets
Wrote all day but had no lockets
Bright with pictures of his Girl.
I know one who loves and parties
And has done so since his thirties
But writes hardly anything at all.

Brothers and Friends

What makes this statue noble-seeming

What makes this statue noble-seeming
Is the emphasis upon
The upper portions of the face
And not the lower ones.
The sensuous mouth
Is scarcely emphasized at all
Rather the eyes and nose
Both of the Intellectual part and not
Too near the animal-seeming
Kiss-conceiving and germ-breathing
Mouth, yet, Grecian girl, it seems to me
You and I are breathing
Not from the architectural head
Or forehead's gradual slope. Instead
We're breathing through the mouth.
I'm out of breath!
I want you! That or death!
I want your mouth, your breath!

Two Worlds

A la Coconut School

A la Coconut School
Tous étaient mayas—
On portait le maya costume
Et puis on avait coûtume
De manger des mets mayas
Et de boire le vin des Indes.

Students, students, demand
When you become woman and man
To revisiter ces écoles
To come back to these schools!
For the best that any life can
Is by the past to make reprimands—
Were we ever just fools?

At the American School
Everyone was American—
In jeans they played it cool
No one was patrician.
They danced the Fourth of July
As the years passed by.

Oh and surely it's good to demand
To return to one's school
Where maybe one teacher was cool
But not more than a rubber band
Where the girls were as tall as the boys
And had mutual sexual joys
Although smoking was contraband
And past one a.m. making noise!

A l'école Coleridge
Everyone was Dorothy Wordsworth
Certains fûrent Keats

And some were Shelley
Mais l'instruction journalière une fois accomplie
Ces identités s'en étaient allées.
But by the end of the teaching day
These identities had gone away.
Gone, gone, gone away
But to be resumed the next day
Dorothy John and Percy Bysshe
Assumed and cast-off, at the teachers' wish!

Oh, to go back to the Schools
With all that we know today!
The teachers we thought were such fools!
The hours and hours of play!
On était un peu ridicule
And went riding about on a mule
With a pleasure undreamed-of today
Bonheur aujourd'hui même pas revé!

How Life Began

A NOTE ON THE TYPE

This book is set in a digital version of *Ehrhardt,* a type face deriving its name from the Ehrhardt type foundry in Frankfurt, Germany. The original design of the face was the work of Nicholas Kis, a Hungarian punch cutter known to have worked in Amsterdam from 1680 to 1689. The modern version of Ehrhardt was cut by The Monotype Corporation of London in 1937.

Composition by NK Graphics, Keene, New Hampshire
Printed at The Stinehour Press, Lunenburg, Vermont
Bound by The Book Press, Brattleboro, Vermont
Designed by Harry Ford